I
Imagine
Angels

Poems and Prayers for Parents and Children

THE METROPOLITAN MUSEUM OF ART
NEW YORK

Atheneum Books for Young Readers
NEW YORK • LONDON • TORONTO • SYDNEY • SINGAPORE

All of the works of art reproduced in this book are from the collections of The Metropolitan Museum of Art.

COVER: *The Adoration of the Shepherds with Saint Catherine of Alexandria* (detail). Cigoli (Ludovico Cardi), Italian, Florence, 1559–1613. Oil on canvas, 10 ft. 1⅜ in. x 6 ft. 4¼ in., 1599.

ENDPAPERS: *Dante and Beatrice with the Blessed Souls* (detail). Woodcut from Dante Alighieri, *Comedia dell'Inferno, del Purgatorio, & del Paradiso* (Canto 27 of *Paradiso*), 5 x 4⅛ in. Venice: Giovambattista, Marchio Sessa, & Fratelli, 1578.

TITLE PAGE: *The Seventh Angel of the Apocalypse Proclaiming the Reign of the Lord* (detail). Leaf from a Beatus manuscript, Spanish, Burgos, about 1180. Tempera, gold, and ink on parchment, 17⅜ x 11⅞ in.

CONTENTS PAGE: *Fame (Angel with Trumpet)*. Luca Cambiaso, Italian, Genoa, 1527–1585. Pen and bistre on paper, 13½ x 9½ in.

BACK FLAP: *Grace Before Meals* from *A Day in a Child's Life*, 1881. Kate Greenaway, British, 1846–1901. London: George Routledge and Sons. Hand-colored wood engraving.

BACK COVER: *Jungle Tales (Contes de la Jungle)*. James Jebusa Shannon, American, 1862–1923. Oil on canvas, 34¼ x 44¾ in., 1895.

Published by The Metropolitan Museum of Art and Atheneum Books for Young Readers

Atheneum Books for Young Readers
An imprint of Simon & Schuster Children's Publishing Division
1230 Avenue of the Americas, New York, New York 10020

Visit the Museum's Web site: www.metmuseum.org
Visit Simon & Schuster's Web site: www.SimonSaysKids.com

Printed in Hong Kong
09 08 07 06 05 04 03 02 01 00   5 4 3 2 1

Produced by the Department of Special Publications, The Metropolitan Museum of Art:
Robie Rogge, Publishing Manager; William Lach, Editor; Anna Raff, Designer; Tatiana Ginsberg, Production Associate.
All photography by The Metropolitan Museum of Art Photograph Studio

Library of Congress Cataloging-in-Publication Data

I imagine angels : poems and prayers for parents and children / edited by William Lach.
    p. cm.
    Summary: Presents a collection of prayers, psalms, and spiritual poetry accompanied by thematically related works of art from the collections of the Metropolitan Museum of Art.
    ISBN 0-87099-949-4 (MMA). — ISBN 0-689-84080-2 (Atheneum)
    1. Religious poetry. 2. Prayers. [1. Religious poetry. 2. Prayers. 3. Poetry—Collections.]
I. Lach, William, 1968– II. Metropolitan Museum of Art (New York, N.Y.)

PN6110.R4 I24 2000
808.81'9382—dc21

                                        00-024836

FIRST EDITION

Contents

Introduction 4

Guillaume Apollinaire *Mirror* 7

Cecil Frances Alexander *All Things Bright and Beautiful* 8–9

Bhagavad Gita *God of the Winds...* 11

William Blake *from Auguries of Innocence* 12

Gwendolyn Brooks *The Preacher...* 15

E. E. Cummings *I Thank You God...* 16

Emily Dickinson *I Never Saw a Moor* 19

Ecclesiastes *To Every Thing There Is a Season* 20

Gerard Manley Hopkins *Pied Beauty* 23

Langston Hughes *Tambourines* 24

Kobayashi Issa *Three Haiku* 27

Jalal-Ud-Din Rumi *The Face of That Angel* 28

Mayan hymn *from The Popul Vuh* 31

Ogden Nash *Morning Prayer* 32

Mary Oliver *Some Questions You Might Ask* 35

Psalm 23 *The Lord Is My Shepherd* 36

St. Richard of Chichester *Day by Day* 39

Tewan prayer *Song of the Sky Loom* 40

Mary Dixon Thayer *A Great Gray Elephant* 43

Traditional prayer *Now I Lay Me Down to Sleep* 44

Walt Whitman *from Song of Myself* 47

Credits 48

Introduction

The word *angel* comes from the Greek word for *messenger*. Most parents and children would probably describe these heavenly spirits in the same way, as couriers of sorts who speed good words to and from God. The angels interspersed throughout this collection convey the spiritual messages of poems, prayers, and art from around the world.

Here, a Zen haiku about the bliss of life during cherry-blossom time reflects a Japanese woodblock print of a girl viewing flowers by lantern light. Langston Hughes's "gospel shout" gives voice to a Romare Bearden collage of an urban angel choir. E. E. Cummings's modern sonnet of thanks for "a blue true dream of sky" echoes the light blue expanse of a Pablo Picasso linoleum print. And the familiar psalm "The Lord Is My Shepherd" is reimagined beside an Italian Renaissance painting of the archangel Raphael taking Tobias by the hand.

It has often been said that there are many ways to pray. With works of art and writing from a multitude of traditions, this collection offers many ways to start.

—William Lach, Editor

The Love Song (detail). Sir Edward Coley Burne-Jones, British, 1833–1898. Oil on canvas, 45 x 61⅛ in.

Mirror

IN THIS

IONS   MIR

FLECT   ROR

RE   I

THE   AM

LIKE   Guillaume   EN

NOT   Apollinaire   CLOSED

AND   A

GELS   LIVE

AN   AND

GINE   REAL

MA   AS

I YOU

—Guillaume Apollinaire
French, 1880–1918
translation Kenneth Koch

Detail of one of two leaves from *The Hours of Chàrles of France*. Master of Charles of France, French, Bourges. Tempera, ink, and gold leaf on vellum, 6¾ x 4⅞ in., 1465.

All Things Bright and Beautiful

All things bright and beautiful,
    All creatures great and small,
All things wise and wonderful,
    The Lord God made them all.

Each little flower that opens,
    Each little bird that sings,
He made their glowing colors,
    He made their shining wings.

The purple-headed mountain,
    The river running by,
The sunset and the morning
    That brighten up the sky.

The cold wind in the winter,
    The pleasant summer sun,
The ripe fruit in the garden,
    He made them every one.

Peaceable Kingdom (detail). Edward Hicks, American, 1780–1849. Oil on canvas, 17⅞ x 23⅞ in., ca. 1830–32.

ISAIAH 11 Chap. 6 & 7

He gave us eyes to see them,
And lips that we might tell
How great is God Almighty
Who has made all things well.

—Cecil Frances Alexander
English, 1823–1895

God of the Winds and the Waters

God of the winds and the waters, of fire and death!
Lord of the solitary moon, the Creator, the Ancestor of all!
Adoration unto thee, a thousand adorations;
and again and again unto thee adoration.

Adoration unto thee who art before me and behind me:
adoration unto thee who art on all sides, God of all.

—from the Bhagavad Gita
translation Juan Mascaró

Bhairavi Ragini. Indian, Punjab Hills, Mandi, ca. 1630–35. Page from a dispersed Ragmala series.
Opaque watercolor, silver, and gold on paper, 10⅛ x 8 in.

from Auguries of Innocence

To see a World in a Grain of Sand
And a Heaven in a Wild Flower,
Hold Infinity in the palm of your hand
And Eternity in an hour.

A Robin Redbreast in a Cage
Puts all Heaven in a Rage.
A dove house fill'd with doves and pigeons
Shudders Hell thro' all its regions.
A dog starv'd at his Master's Gate
Predicts the ruin of the State.
A Horse misus'd upon the Road
Calls to Heaven for Human blood.
Each outcry of the hunted Hare
A fibre from the Brain does tear.
A Skylark wounded in the wing,
A Cherubim does cease to sing.

—William Blake
English, 1757–1827

Frontispiece to *Songs of Experience*, 1789. William Blake, British, 1757–1827. Hand-colored relief etching, 4⅜ x 2⅝ in.

The Preacher: Ruminates Behind the Sermon

I think it must be lonely to be God.
Nobody loves a master. No. Despite
The bright hosannas, bright dear-Lords, and bright
Determined reverence of Sunday eyes.

Picture Jehovah striding through the hall
Of His importance, creatures running out
From servant-corners to acclaim, to shout
Appreciation of His merit's glare.

But who walks with Him?—dares to take His arm,
To slap Him on the shoulder, tweak His ear,
Buy Him a Coca-Cola or a beer,
Pooh-pooh His politics, call Him a fool?

Perhaps—who knows?—He tires of looking down.
Those eyes are never lifted. Never straight.
Perhaps sometimes He tires of being great
In solitude. Without a hand to hold.

—Gwendolyn Brooks
American, b. 1917

Her World (detail). Philip Evergood, American, 1901–1973. Oil on canvas, 48 x 35⅝ in., 1948.

I Thank You God for Most This Amazing

i thank You God for most this amazing
day:for the leaping greenly spirits of trees
and a blue true dream of sky;and for everything
which is natural which is infinite which is yes

(i who have died am alive again today,
and this is the sun's birthday;this is the birth
day of life and of love and wings:and of the gay
great happening illimitably earth)

how should tasting touching hearing seeing
breathing any—lifted from the no
of all nothing—human merely being
doubt unimaginable You?

(now the ears of my ears awake and
now the eyes of my eyes are opened)

—E. E. Cummings
American, 1894–1962

Bacchanalia with a Black Bull. Pablo Picasso, Spanish, 1881–1973. Linoleum cut, 20¼ x 25¼ in., 1959.

I Never Saw a Moor

I never saw a moor,
I never saw the sea;
Yet know I how the heather looks,
And what a wave must be.

I never spoke with God,
Nor visited in heaven;
Yet certain am I of the spot
As if the chart were given.

—Emily Dickinson
American, 1830–1886

To Every Thing There Is a Season

To every thing there is a season, and a time to every purpose under the heaven:
a time to be born, and a time to die; a time to plant, and a time to pluck up
    that which is planted;
a time to kill, and a time to heal; a time to break down, and a time to build up;
a time to weep, and a time to laugh; a time to mourn, and a time to dance;
a time to cast away stones, and a time to gather stones together; a time to
    embrace, and a time to refrain from embracing;
a time to get, and a time to lose; a time to keep, and a time to cast away;
a time to rend, and a time to sew; a time to keep silence, and a time to speak;
a time to love, and a time to hate; a time of war, and a time of peace.

—Ecclesiastes 3:1–8

The Months of the Year (detail). English, second quarter 17th century. Embroidered textile. Colored wool, silk, and silver thread on canvas, 20½ x 22¼ in.

Pied Beauty

Glory be to God for dappled things—
    For skies of couple-colour as a brinded cow;
      For rose-moles all in stipple upon trout that swim;
Fresh-firecoal chestnut-falls; finches' wings;
    Landscape plotted and pieced—fold, fallow, and plough;
      And áll trádes, their gear and tackle and trim.

All things counter, original, spare, strange;
    Whatever is fickle, freckled (who knows how?)
      With swift, slow; sweet, sour; adazzle, dim;
He fathers-forth whose beauty is past change:
                Praise him.

—Gerard Manley Hopkins
English, 1844–1889

July Hay (detail). Thomas Hart Benton, American, 1889–1975. Egg tempera, methyl cellulose, and oil on Masonite, 38 x 26¾ in., 1943.

Tambourines

Tambourines!
Tambourines!
Tambourines
To the glory of God!
Tambourines
To glory!

A gospel shout
And a gospel song:
Life is short
But God is long!

Tambourines!
Tambourines!
Tambourines
To glory!

—Langston Hughes
American, 1902–1967

Three Haiku

What a strange thing!
to be alive
    beneath cherry blossoms.

    All the time I pray to Buddha
I keep on
    killing mosquitoes.

Only birds
sing the music of heaven
    in this world.

—Kobayashi Issa
Japanese, 1763–1827
translation Robert Hass

Girl Viewing Plum Blossoms at Night. Suzuki Harunobu, Japanese, 1725–1770. Polychrome woodblock print, (ōban) 12¾ x 8¼ in., ca. 1768.

The Face of That Angel

The face of that angel
    landed in my heart.
Is there anyone as happy as me?—
I truly cannot say.

I hear about sorrow
But have no idea what it is.

—Jalal-Ud-Din Rumi
Persian, 1207–1273
translation Jonathan Star and Shahram Shiva

Bahram Gur Visits the Persian Princess in the Purple Palace in the Sixth Paradise (detail). Attributed to Manohar, Indian, Mughal, period of Akbar (r. 1556–1605).
Leaf from a *Khamsa* (Five Poems) by Amir Khusrau of Delhi. Ink, colors, and gold on paper, 9¾ x 6¼ in., ca. 1595.

from The Popul Vuh

Truly now,
double thanks, triple thanks
that we've been formed, we've been given
our mouths, our faces,
we speak, we listen,
we wonder, we move,
our knowledge is good, we've understood
what is far and near,
and we've seen what is great and small
under the sky, on the earth.

—Mayan hymn
translation Dennis Tedlock

Detail of a plate with trumpeter. Mexican or Guatemalan, Maya, 8th century. Polychrome ceramic, Diam. 12¾ in.

Morning Prayer

Now another day is breaking,
Sleep was sweet and so is waking.
Dear Lord, I promised you last night
Never again to sulk or fight.
Such vows are easier to keep
When a child is sound asleep.
Today, O Lord, for your dear sake,
I'll try to keep them when awake.

—Ogden Nash
American, 1902–1971

Frances and Charles Cowdrey (detail). Henry Walton, American, 1804–1865.
Watercolor, gouache, black chalk, and graphite on off-white wove paper, 11¼ x 12⅜ in., ca. 1839.

Some Questions You Might Ask

Is the soul solid, like iron?
Or is it tender and breakable, like
the wings of a moth in the beak of the owl?
Who has it, and who doesn't?
I keep looking around me.
The face of the moose is as sad
as the face of Jesus.
The swan opens her white wings slowly.
In the fall, the black bear carries leaves into the darkness.
One question leads to another.
Does it have a shape? Like an iceberg?
Like the eye of a hummingbird?
Does it have one lung, like the snake and the scallop?
Why should I have it, and not the anteater
who loves her children?
Why should I have it, and not the camel?
Come to think of it, what about the maple trees?
What about the blue iris?
What about all the little stones, sitting alone in the moonlight?
What about roses, and lemons, and their shining leaves?
What about the grass?

—Mary Oliver
American, b. 1935

Jungle Tales (Contes de la Jungle) (detail). James Jebusa Shannon, American, 1862–1923. Oil on canvas, 34¼ x 44¾ in., 1895.

The Lord Is My Shepherd

The Lord is my shepherd; I shall not want.

He maketh me to lie down in green pastures:
   he leadeth me beside the still waters.

He restoreth my soul: he leadeth me in the
   paths of righteousness for his name's sake.

Yea, though I walk through the valley of the
   shadow of death, I will fear no evil: for
   thou art with me; thy rod and thy staff
   they comfort me.

Thou preparest a table before me in the presence
   of mine enemies: thou anointest my head
   with oil; my cup runneth over.

Surely goodness and mercy shall follow me
   all the days of my life: and I will dwell in
   the house of the Lord forever.

—Psalm 23

The Archangel Raphael and Tobias. Neri di Bicci, Italian, Florence, 1419–1491. Tempera on panel, 11⅞ x 9⅟₁₆ in.

Day by Day

Day by day, dear Lord of Thee
Three things I pray:
    To see Thee more clearly,
    To love Thee more dearly,
    To follow Thee more nearly,
      Day by day.

—St. Richard of Chichester
English, 1197–1253

Grace Before Meals from *A Day in a Child's Life*, 1881. Kate Greenaway, British, 1846–1901. London: George Routledge and Sons. Hand-colored wood engraving.

Song of the Sky Loom

O Our Mother the Earth, O Our Father the Sky
Your children are we and with tired backs
We bring you the gifts you love.
Then weave for us a garment of brightness
May the warp be the white light of morning
May the weft be the red light of evening
May the fringes be the falling rain
May the border be the standing rainbow.
Thus weave for us a garment of brightness
That we may walk fittingly where the grass is green
O Our Mother the Earth, O Our Father the Sky.

—Tewan prayer
translation Herbert Spinden

The Rocky Mountains, Lander's Peak (detail). Albert Bierstadt, American, 1830–1902. Oil on canvas, 6 ft. 1½ in. x 10 ft. ¾ in., 1863.

A Great Gray Elephant

A great gray elephant,
A little yellow bee,
A tiny purple violet,
    A tall green tree,
A red and white sailboat
On a blue sea—
All these things
You gave to me,
When you made
My eyes to see—
    Thank you, God!

—Mary Dixon Thayer
American, 1896–1989

Prince Riding on an Elephant. Khemkaran, Indian, Mughal, period of Akbar (r. 1556–1605). Ink, opaque watercolor, and gold on paper, 6⅛ x 7⅞ in.

Now I Lay Me Down to Sleep

Now I lay me down to sleep,
I pray Thee, Lord, thy child to keep:
Thy love guard me through the night
And wake me with the morning light.
                                        Amen.

—Traditional prayer

Asleep. Horace Pippin, American, 1888–1946. Oil on canvas board, 9 x 12 in., 1943.

from Song of Myself

Why should I wish to see God better than this day?
I see something of God each hour of the twenty-four, and each moment then,
In the faces of men and women I see God, and in my own face in the glass,
I find letters from God dropt in the street, and every one is sign'd by God's name,
And I leave them where they are, for I know that wheresoe'er I go,
Others will punctually come for ever and ever.

—Walt Whitman
American, 1819–1892

Paradise (detail). Giovanni di Paolo, Italian, Sienna, active by 1417, died 1482. Tempera and gold on canvas, transferred from wood, 18½ x 16 in.

Credits

Cover: Gwynne Andrews Fund, 1991 1991.7. Endpapers: Gift of Francis Leonard Cater, 1958 58.584. Title page: Purchase, The Cloisters Collection, Rogers and Harris Brisbane Dick Funds, and Joseph Pulitzer Bequest, 1991 1991.232.12. Contents page: Robert Lehman Collection, 1975 1975.1.283. Page 5: The Alfred N. Punnett Endowment Fund, 1947 47.26. Page 6: The Cloisters Collection, 1958 58.71a. Pages 8–9: Gift of Edgar William and Bernice Chrysler Garbisch, 1970 1970.283.1. Page 10: Rogers Fund, 1958 58.1.1. Page 13: Rogers Fund, 1917 17.10.28. Page 14: Arthur Hoppock Hearn Fund, 1950 50.29. Page 17: The Mr. and Mrs. Charles Kramer Collection, Gift of Mr. and Mrs. Charles Kramer, 1985 1985.1079.3. Page 18: Jacques and Natasha Gelman Collection, 1998 1999.363.3. Page 21: Gift of Irwin Untermyer, 1964 64.101.1324. Page 22: George A. Hearn Fund, 1943 43.159.1. Page 25: Gift of Mr. and Mrs. Samuel Shore, 1978 1978.61.2. Page 26: Fletcher Fund, 1929 JP 1506. Page 29: Gift of Alexander Smith Cochran, 1913 13.228.33. Page 30: Gift of Eugene and Ina Schnell, 1989 1989.110. Page 33: Gift of Edgar William and Bernice Chrysler Garbisch, 1966 66.242.12. Page 34: Arthur Hoppock Hearn Fund, 1913 13.143.1. Page 37: Robert Lehman Collection, 1975 1975.1.71. Page 38: Rogers Fund, 1921 21.36.91. Page 41: Rogers Fund, 1907 07.123. Page 42: Rogers Fund, 1925 25.68.4. Page 45: Bequest of Jane Kendall Gingrich, 1982 1982.55.3. Page 46: Rogers Fund, 1906 06.1046. Back flap: Rogers Fund, 1921 21.36.91. Back cover: Arthur Hoppock Hearn Fund, 1913 13.143.1.

Grateful acknowledgment is made to the following for permission to reprint the copyrighted material listed below. "Mirror," by Guillaume Apollinaire, translation copyright © 1998 by Kenneth Koch, reprinted by permission of the translator, from *Making Your Own Days/The Pleasures of Reading and Writing Poetry* (Simon & Schuster). "God of the Winds," from the Bhagavad Gita, translated by Juan Mascaró, copyright © 1962 by Juan Mascaró, reproduced by permission of Penguin Books Ltd. "The Preacher: Ruminates Behind the Sermon," by Gwendolyn Brooks, copyright © by Gwendolyn Brooks, reprinted by permission of the author. "i thank You God for most this amazing," copyright © 1950, 1978, 1991 by the Trustees for the E. E. Cummings Trust. Copyright © 1979 George James Firmage, from *Complete Poems: 1904–1962* by E. E. Cummings, edited by George J. Firmage. Used by permission of Liveright Publishing Corporation. "Tambourines," from *Collected Poems* by Langston Hughes, copyright © 1994 by the Estate of Langston Hughes. Reprinted by permission of Alfred A. Knopf, a Division of Random House, Inc. "What a strange thing," "All the time," and "Only birds" by Kobayashi Issa, from *The Essential Haiku: Versions of Basho, Buson, & Issa*, edited and with an introduction by Robert Hass, translation copyright © 1994 by Robert Hass, reprinted by permission of HarperCollins Publishers, Inc. "The Face of That Angel," by Jalal-Ud-Din Rumi, translated by Jonathan Star and Shahram Shiva, copyright © 1992 by Jonathan Star, from the book *A Garden Beyond Paradise: The Mystical Poetry of Rumi*, reprinted by permission of the translators. Excerpt from *Popul Vuh: The Definitive Edition of the Mayan Book of the Dawn of Life and the Glories of Gods and Kings*, translated by Dennis Tedlock, copyright © 1985, 1996 by Dennis Tedlock, reprinted with the permission of Simon & Schuster. "Morning Prayer," from *Custard and Company* by Ogden Nash, copyright © 1961, 1962 by Ogden Nash, reprinted by permission of Little, Brown and Company (Inc.). "Some Questions You Might Ask," copyright © 1990 by Mary Oliver, from *House of Light*, reprinted by permission of Beacon Press, Boston. "A Great Gray Elephant," from *The Child on His Knees* by Mary Dixon Thayer, copyright © 1926 by Macmillan Publishing Company, renewed 1954 by Mary D. T. Fremont-Smith, reprinted with the permission of Scribner, a Division of Simon & Schuster.

Girl at a Window, by Balthus, copyright © 2000 by Artists Rights Society (ARS), New York/ADAGP, Paris. *The Block*, by Romare Bearden, copyright © 2000 by Romare Bearden Foundation/VAGA, NY, NY. *July Hay*, by Thomas Hart Benton, copyright © 2000 by T. H. Benton and R. P. Benton Testamentary Trusts/ VAGA, NY, NY. *Bacchanalia with a Black Bull*, by Pablo Picasso, copyright © 2000 by the Estate of Pablo Picasso/Artists Rights Society (ARS), New York.